13 Modern Artists
Children Should Know

Brad Finger

PRESTEL

Munich · London · New York

Contents

13 modern artists changed forever the way people see and understand art. They painted objects and people in new ways. They made sculptures with materials that had never been used before. Some even began planting trees as a form of art!

This book talks about 13 of the most important modern artists, and it shows you some of their best creations. The glossary at the back of the book explains words that you may not know. Each of these words is marked with an asterisk*.

A timeline shows what was happening in the world when the artists lived. There are also some quiz questions about the art that you see here. If you want to learn more about an artist, we have tips for further reading, places to visit, and web addresses that will help you. If you want to make your own modern art, we have some fun suggestions for how you can do it.

Happy reading …
and be sure to explore your own creativity!

1914-18 First World War
Marc Chagall 1887-1985
Pablo Picasso 1881-1973
Marcel Duchamp 1887-1968

1898 Spain loses the last of its American Empire in the Spanish-American War

1865   1870   1875   1880   1885   1890   1895   1900   1905   1910   1915   19

Maya with Doll, 1938
Musée Picasso, Paris

Pablo had a way of making portraits that was all his own. Look at this painting of Picasso's daughter Maya. The artist made one of her eyes lower than the other, and he pushed her nose and mouth over to the side! Yet even though Maya's portrait was imaginary in many ways, it still looked a little bit like the real girl.

Tip:
The Museum Picasso in Barcelona has one of the best collections of Picasso's art in the world. Pablo spent much of his early life in Barcelona.

Pablo Picasso— The Modern Revolution

He is the most famous modern artist. Picasso painted with his imagination, and many other artists followed his example.

Young Pablo showed a great talent for painting. At the age of seven, he began taking art lessons from his father, Jose, who was also a painter. Pablo learned how to draw people just as they appeared in real life.

But as he grew older, Picasso wanted to paint differently. He liked the carefree, creative way that young children drew pictures. These pictures, Picasso felt, captured the spirit of the objects they portrayed better than realistic art did.

So Pablo began teaching himself how to paint like a child, using his imagination. In 1900, he visited Paris for the first time. Many of the most important artists lived and worked there, and Picasso soon made many new friends. A few years later, Pablo and a few other painters developed the first important style of modern art, called Cubism*. In Cubist paintings, the images often look like they have been broken up into small geometric shapes.

Throughout his life, Pablo would master different artistic styles. He would even learn to sculpt. Yet all of his art had a certain look that only Picasso could create.

Pablo lived to the old age of 91, and he never stopped making art.

Born:
  25 October 1881
  in Málaga, Spain
Died:
  8 April 1973 in
  Mougins, France
Lived in:
  Málaga, La Coruña,
  Barcelona, Madrid,
  Paris, Aix-en-
  Provence, Mougins
Painting styles:
  Cubism*, but he tried
  many other styles
Children:
  Paola, Maya, Claude,
  Paloma
Hobby:
  Bullfighting

✳ 1889 The Eiffel Tower is completed for the Paris World's Fair

Pablo Picasso 1881-1973

Edward Hopper 1882-1967

Marcel Duchamp 1887-1968

1914-18 First World War

| 1870 | 1875 | 1880 | 1885 | 1890 | 1895 | 1900 | 1905 | 1910 | 1915 | 1920 | 19 |

Born:
28 July 1887 in
Blainville-Crevon,
France
Died:
2 October 1968
in Paris, France
Lived in:
Blainville-Crevon,
Paris, New York City
Painting styles:
Dadaism*, Surrealism*
Hobby:
Chess

Marcel Duchamp — The Game of Art

He could create surprising and often funny works of art out of ordinary objects: from a bicycle wheel to a toilet!

Marcel Duchamp grew up in a family that loved art and loved games. His sister Suzanne became a famous painter, and Marcel enjoyed playing games with Suzanne when he was a child.

As an adult, Duchamp made art by playing games with everyday objects. Once, he decided to place an ordinary bicycle wheel on top of an ordinary stool. When these two objects were joined in that way, they made an extraordinary looking creation. Another time, Duchamp turned a simple bathroom toilet upside-down so that the back part of it rested on the ground and the front part stuck straight up in the air. The toilet now looked a little like a drinking fountain, and Marcel called it *Fountain*. Both *Bicycle Wheel* and *Fountain* became famous works of art.

Many people who first saw Duchamp's creations hated them. "How could someone put a toilet in an art gallery and call it art?" they asked angrily. But other people found these works funny and meaningful, and they agreed with Marcel that art could be more than just paintings and sculptures. Artists called Surrealists* and Dadaists* soon made other artworks by showing ordinary things in new and creative ways.

As he grew older, Marcel stopped making art and began writing about it. He also promoted the work of other important artists, like Alexander Calder. Duchamp helped make modern art popular around the world.

**Bicycle Wheel, 1951
(third version, after lost
original of 1913)**
Museum of Modern Art,
New York

One of Duchamp's most
famous early creations is
Bicycle Wheel, from 1913.
Duchamp made the
sculpture by placing a
bicycle wheel on top of a
stool. It almost looks like
a small person standing
on spindly legs! People
later called this kind of
artwork a "readymade."
Readymades consist
of things that were not
actually produced by
the artist.

Good to know:
Marcel Duchamp loved
to play games, and he
became a great chess
player. Duchamp earned
the title of chess master,
meaning he could beat
some of the best chess
players in the world. Do
you know how to play
chess?

Further reading:
*Marcel Duchamp: A Life
in Pictures* by Jennifer
Gough-Cooper.

Edward Hopper 1882-1967

Marc Chagall 1887-1985
Marcel Duchamp 1887-1968

1917 Russian Revolution

1914-18 First World War

1922 The Soviet Union is founded

1880　　1885　　1890　　1895　　1900　　1905　　1910　　1915　　1920　　1925　　1930　　19

The Juggler, 1943
Collection Gilbert W.
Chapman, New York

A Chagall painting is
often like a mysterious
carnival. This picture is
called *The Juggler*. In it,
a half-human, half-bird
creature kicks its leg
up in the air and seems
to "juggle" the other
characters around it.
Look closely … and you
can see a tiny horse and
rider from the circus, a
country fiddler, and a
beautiful ballet dancer.
The bird-person also has
a clock hanging over its
arm. Perhaps this clock
symbolizes the fact that
a carnival—and a human
life—will not last forever.

Marc Chagall—Childhood Dreams

Chagall grew up in a small village, and the people and way of life from his childhood would always play an important role in his art.

Born: 7 July 1887 in
  Vitebsk, Belarus
Died:
  28 March 1985 in Saint-
  Paul-de-Vence, France
Lived in:
  Vitebsk, St. Petersburg,
  Moscow, Paris, New
  York, High Falls (NY),
  Vence, Saint-Paul-de-
  Vence
Children:
  Ida, David
Painting styles:
  Expressionism*,
  Surrealism*

Young Marc Chagall enjoyed watching the people of his village carry out their daily tasks. They milked cows, they harvested wheat, and they brought food to sell at the market. Marc's own father sold fish. Though they were poor and had to work hard, the people in Marc's village made time to dance, play music, and have fun.

Young Marc showed a talent for drawing, and his parents sent him to a teacher in the village so that he could learn to paint. Chagall learned quickly. He soon moved to St. Petersburg, then the Russian capital city, to continue his studies. A few years later, he moved to Paris, the capital of the art world at that time.

When Marc painted, he liked to include things that he remembered from his childhood. He painted cows, chickens, and lambs; and he also painted farmers and country musicians. Yet Chagall's animals and people do not resemble those from real life. Some are green or purple in color, while others are painted upside-down instead of right side up. Marc's strange creatures often appear to float and dance, as if they are living in a happy dream world!

People loved Chagall's joyful pictures, and the artist's popularity and fame grew. In his later life, Marc learned to create artworks other than paintings. He made stained glass windows for cathedrals, mosaics* for city squares, and illustrations for picture books.

The Blue Circus, 1950-52
Centre Georges
Pompidou, Paris

Chagall loved circuses.
As a young man in Paris,
he often went to see the
circus with his friends.
This picture shows a
daring female trapeze
artist on her trapeze.
But is she flying though
the air or moving through
the water? The deep blue
background could be a
night sky, with a shining
moon. But it could also
be the ocean, with a fish
swimming by.
What do you think you see
in the painting?

Quiz:
Fish appear in many of
Marc Chagall's paintings.
Why did Chagall paint
fish so often?
(Answer on p. 46)

The Birthday, 1915
Museum of Modern Art,
New York

Chagall's dreamlike
people often express
their feelings better
than real-looking people
could do. Here, a floating
man shows his love for
a woman by twisting his
neck all the way around
to kiss her.

What things from your life would you put in a drawing? Would you include
a favorite pet, or maybe something you remember from a fun vacation?
Think about several things that are important to you and try to draw them
in an unusual way.

Born:
22 July 1882 in Nyack, New York, USA

Died:
15 May 1967 in New York City, USA

Lived in:
Nyack, New York City, South Truro (MA)

Painting style:
Realism*

Interest:
Reading

Tip:
The childhood home of Edward Hopper in Nyack, New York is now a museum where you can learn about the painter. It is called the Edward Hopper House Art Center. The museum is also a place where new artists can study with teachers and show their own creations.

Further reading:
Edward Hopper: Summer at the Seashore by Deborah Lyons (Prestel's *Adventures in Art* series).

Edward Hopper — The American Scene

He painted his country the way he saw it. Hopper's America was a big place where people could travel for miles on distant roads and explore huge cities like New York. But it was also a lonely and sometimes sad place.

Edward was a late bloomer. He learned to paint as a child, but he spent a long time figuring out exactly how he wanted to paint. As a young man, Edward needed to make money to support himself, so he made drawings to illustrate magazines and newspapers. Other people told Edward what to draw for these illustrations. But Hopper didn't enjoy working for others. He wanted to be an artist, and artists should decide for themselves what their art should be about.

During the 1920's, when Edward was in his forties, he finally developed his own unique way of painting. Many modern artists who were Edward's age painted unreal things that came from their imagination. But Edward painted things as he saw them in the real world. He liked to paint buildings and city streets; he liked to paint people eating in restaurants and going to movie theaters; and he liked to paint countryroads and seaside towns. He also liked to show the way light—especially sunlight—shines on people and objects, and how it creates beautiful colors.

Lighthouse Hill, 1927
Dallas Museum of Art,
Dallas

During the summertime,
Hopper lived in a small
New England town by
the sea. He sometimes
painted the nearby
lighthouses that helped
guide ships to shore.
In this picture, called
Lighthouse Hill, Hopper
makes the buildings look
isolated and far away.
The soft evening sunlight
even makes them seem
lonely.

Edward painted people, objects, and light in a particular way. The people in Hopper's art don't always look happy, and they often seem bored. Even his buildings and landscapes can look sad. Hopper showed that people in the modern world can feel lonely, even if they live in a big city.

Gas, 1940
Museum of Modern Art, New York

Hopper often shows people in quiet moments. Here a country gas station owner seems to be closing up his business for the night. It doesn't look like he's had too many customers.

1903 The Wright Brothers fly the first airplane

1914-18 First World War
Alexander Calder 1898-1976
Edward Hopper 1882-1967

Mark Rothko 1903-1970
1915 World's Fair held in San Francisco, USA

1880   1885   1890   1895   1900   1905   1910   1915   1920   1925   1930   19

Born:
  22 July 1898
  in Lawnton,
  Pennsylvania, USA
Died:
  11 November 1976 in
  New York City, USA
Lived in:
  Lawnton, Pasadena
  (CA), San Francisco,
  New York City, Paris
Art style:
  Surrealism*
Children:
  Sandra, Mary
Interests:
  Theater, Ballet

Alexander Calder—Moving Art

He loved things that moved, and he made moving things into art.

Alexander was a chip off the old block. His father was a sculptor, and he wanted to be a sculptor too. When he was 11 years old, Alexander gave his parents a Christmas present—a beautiful duck made out of pieces of metal. But this wasn't an ordinary toy duck. This duck could move back and forth if you tapped it on the head. Ever since that Christmas day, Calder would enjoy making things that moved.

When Alexander grew up, he decided to work as a sculptor in Paris, the center of the art world. Calder first made artwork that looked like real things. He even created an entire miniature circus! But around the year 1930, he became interested in simple shapes. Calder cut pieces of metal into thin, curved forms that could twist easily in the air. He then attached these shapes to a "skeleton" of metal wires, and hung the wire skeleton from the ceiling. When his delicate sculptures hung in the air, they could move in various ways.

La Grande Vitesse, 1969
Calder Plaza,
Grand Rapids, Michigan

Planted firmly in the ground, Calder's huge stabiles look like they could jump up and pounce on an unsuspecting passer-by. This red stabile is named *High Speed*.

The entire sculpture could spin in one direction, while the individual metal pieces could twist in different directions at the same time. Calder's artist friends admired these creations and called them mobiles.

Alexander soon became famous, and he produced mobiles in many different materials and shapes. Later in his life, he started making large sculptures called stabiles for city squares and parks. His stabiles are designed carefully so that their big, curving bodies can rest on thin legs without falling over. Many of the stabiles look almost like huge spiders or crabs!

Mobile
National Gallery of Art, Washington

Calder´s mobiles can resemble delicate tree branches. This small mobile is a model for a huge sculpture in Washington, D.C. Calder used models to work out how the final artwork should look and move.

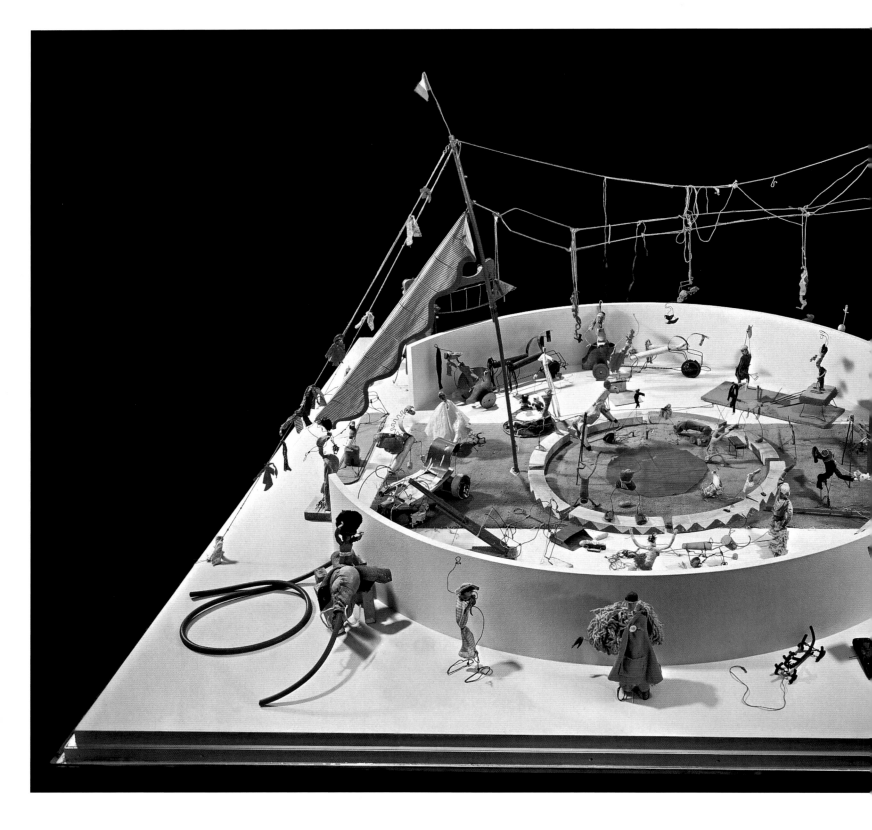

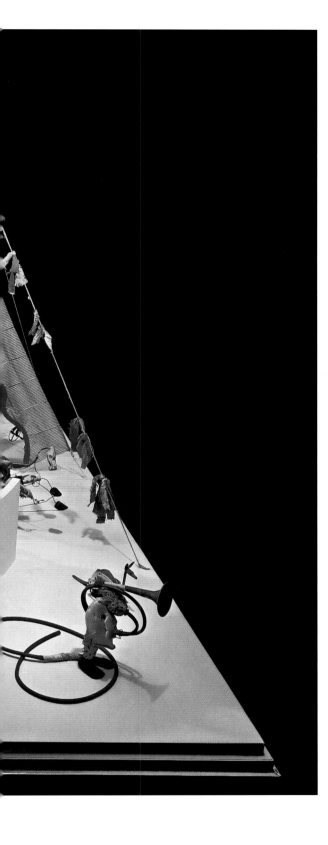

Circus, 1926-31
Whitney Museum of
American Art, New York

The first artwork that
brought Calder fame was
his miniature circus. It
consisted of lions, trapeze
artists, and other circus
characters made out of
metal. Calder attached the
characters to metal wires
so that he could move
them around, almost as a
puppeteer moves puppets.

Tip:
You can go to the web-
site www.calder.org to
see more pictures of
Calder's work, and to
see old photographs of
the artist at work.

1929-41 The Great Depression
Mark Rothko 1903-1970
Alexander Calder 1898-1976
Pablo Picasso 1881-1973

1914-18 First World War   1918-40 Latvia is an independent country for a short time

1900   1905   1910   1912   1914   1916   1918   1920   1925   1930   1932   19

No. 12 (Yellow, Orange, Red on Orange), 1954
Collection Kate Rothko Prizel

Rothko's fuzzy, rectangular shapes seem to float on the canvas. But their meaning is often a mystery. What do you see in this painting?

Good to know:
When Rothko moved to America as a child, he traveled by boat. Mark and other immigrants* went through a place called Ellis Island near New York City. People at Ellis Island had to check the immigrants to make sure they were healthy and didn't have any other problems that would keep them from entering the United States.

Mark Rothko—Color and Form

He painted mysterious shapes and colors, images that could mean many different things to different people.

Born:
  25 September 1903
  in Daugavpils, Latvia
Died:
  25 February 1970 in
  New York City, USA
Lived in:
  Daugavpils, Portland
  (OR), New York City
Painting style:
  Abstract
  Expressionism*
Children:
  Kate, Christopher

Mark Rothko was never satisfied with himself. No matter how hard he worked, nothing ever pleased him. Rothko was born in Latvia, and his original name was Marcus Rothkowitz. Marcus moved to America in 1913, at the age of 10. But he had a hard time making friends in his new country. He felt like a foreigner who never fit in.

Marcus was always searching for happiness, constantly changing things in his life. He worked in a clothing factory for a time. He even tried to become an actor! When these jobs didn't work out, he started painting. But he could never find his own style. Marcus even changed his name to Mark Rothko, which he thought sounded more American.

In the 1940s, World War II began and the United States went to war. The United States and its allies won the war, but the fighting caused terrible things to happen. Cites were bombed and destroyed, and millions of innocent people were killed. When the war ended in 1945, Mark and other artists began to create new styles of painting for a changed world.

Rothko´s new paintings showed fuzzy rectangles of different, carefully chosen colors. Many people admired Rothko´s art. Some found the rectangles to be quiet and relaxing, like floating clouds. Others thought the shapes resembled violent forces of nature, like earthquakes. Rothko let people come up with their own ways of understanding his artwork.

Mark Rothko had finally become a famous painter, but he would never be content with himself. He committed suicide in 1970.

🌸 1933 The Nazis come to power in Germany 🌸 1943 Düsseldorf is heavily bombed 🌸 1949 West Germany is founded

Joseph Beuys 1921-1986
Roy Lichtenstein 1923-1997

Yves Klein 1928-1962
1939-45 Second World War

| 1920 | 1925 | 1930 | 1935 | 1940 | 1942 | 1944 | 1946 | 1948 | 1950 | 1952 | 19 |

Born:
   12 May 1921 in
   Krefeld, Germany
Died:
   23 January 1986 in
   Düsseldorf, Germany
Lived in:
   Krefeld, Kleve
   (Germany),
   Düsseldorf
Art style:
   Post-modernism
Hobby:
   Politics

Joseph Beuys—Risk Taker

He was both an artist and an actor, and he often performed his art. Beuys also showed people how important it was to understand and respect nature.

Joseph Beuys liked to take risks. He fought in the German air force during World War II, nearly dying in a plane crash. Germany lost the war, and Beuys had to overcome poverty and hardship. He did so by taking risks as an artist.

Beuys believed that artists themselves could be part of their own artwork. So he helped create a new kind of art called performance art*. Beuys performed for people like an actor performs in a play. His performances took place in art galleries and museum rooms, and they lasted a long time. The artist would speak and move in carefully chosen ways. He also clothed himself in unusual materials—sometimes with thin pieces of gold and other times with big blankets. Once, he even performed with a live coyote!

Beuys also believed that people should have more respect for nature. One of his most famous performances was called *7,000 Oaks*. In it, he invited many people to help him plant 7,000 trees in the German city of Kassel. Many of the trees were planted in straight lines along city streets, and the project took years to complete. Beuys felt that the tree planting was a kind of art, and that the people who helped him were artists themselves.

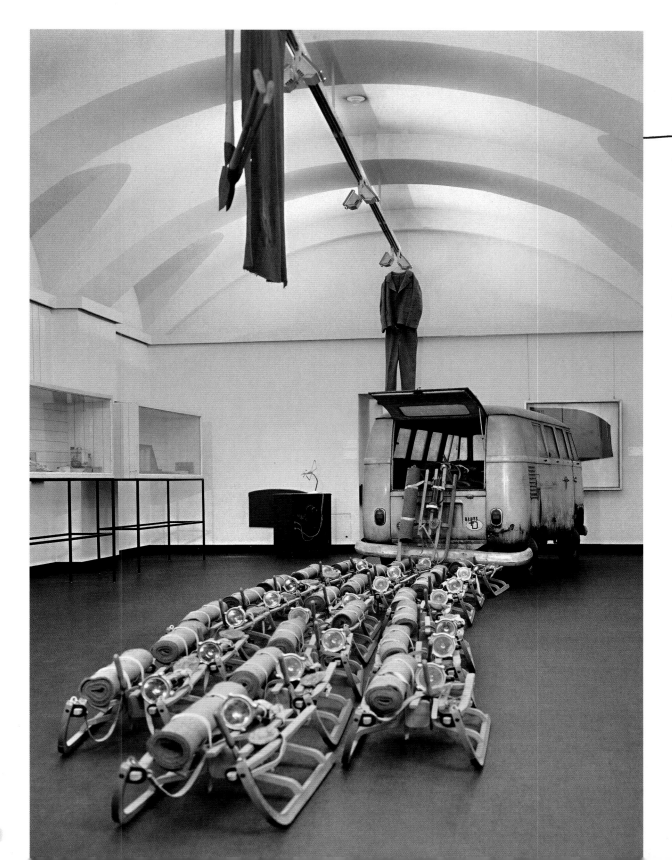

The Pack, 1969
Neue Galerie, Kassel

Joseph Beuys felt that people relied too much on cars and other modern, man-made things. In this sculpture, called *The Pack*, Beuys makes us think about what might happen if things in the modern world stop working. A group of sleds seems to be spilling out of an old, broken-down van. Each of the sleds has a blanket and a flashlight, things people will need if they have to spend the night sleeping outdoors!

7000 Oaks, 1982
Kassel

In his *7,000 Oaks* project from the 1980s, Beuys made the act of planting trees into a work of art. He and his volunteers planted 7,000 trees in and around the city of Kassel, Germany. Today, the oaks still stand in Kassel, reminding people of what Beuys and his fellow artists had done.

Quiz:
How long did it take Beuys and his helpers to plant the 7,000 trees in Kassel?

(Answer on p. 46)

24

Good to know:
Beuys had a life-long interest in nature. Before he became a famous artist, he helped his friend Heinz Sielmann make movies about plants and animals.

1934 First American comic book produced
Roy Lichtenstein 1923-1997
Eva Hesse 1936-1970
Yves Klein 1928-1962
1939-45 Second World War
1950-53 US fights in the Korean

1910   1920   1925   1930   1935   1940   1942   1944   1946   1948   1950   19

**M-Maybe
(A Girl's Picture), 1965**
Museum Ludwig,
Cologne

Lichtenstein used the glamorous people in his art to poke fun at comic book characters. For example, he would make the people think or say silly things that didn't make sense. The woman in this painting may look like a comic book heroine, but she doesn't think like one!

Roy Lichtenstein—Action Hero!

Is it a painting or a comic book? Lichtenstein's funny art often makes people smile, just as real comic books do.

Whaam! Blam! Boom! … The enemy is vanquished by the daring hero! Roy Lichtenstein read comic books as a child, and he loved the way they looked and the thrilling stories they told.

Roy decided to become a painter when he was in college. At first, he tried many different painting styles, but none of them seemed quite right. Then in about 1960, Roy started to make paintings that looked like the comic books from his childhood. Lichtenstein was one of many artists at that time who were developing a style called Pop Art*. Pop Art artists take ordinary things that are easy to understand and well-loved—like comic books—and use them in their artworks.

Roy's comic book paintings showed exciting battles, with airplanes exploding in the air and tanks firing their guns. They also showed beautiful men and women and dramatic city scenes.

Lichtenstein colored his paintings in the same way that comic book makers colored their pictures. He placed tiny colored dots close together on the canvas. When you stood away from the painting, the dots often appeared to make unbroken colors.

Soon everyone wanted to buy Roy's paintings, and Lichtenstein became famous. Even today, he is still among the best loved of all modern artists.

Born:
  27 October 1923 in New York City, USA
Died:
  29 September 1997 in New York City, USA
Lived in:
  New York City, Columbus (OH), Cleveland, Oswego (NY), New Brunswick (NJ)
Painting style:
  Pop Art*
Children:
  David, Mitchell

Whaam!, 1963
Tate Modern, London

Ready, aim, fire! Lichtenstein's famous painting *Whaam!* is based on an actual comic book illustration. Battles like this one look exciting in comic books, but they're pretty scary in real life!

Draw and color your own comic story.

Tip:
To see more Lichtenstein
paintings, visit the website
www.lichtensteinfoundation.org.
This site also has pictures of
Lichtenstein's sculptures.

1939-45 Second World War

Joseph Beuys 1921-1986

Yves Klein 1928-1962

1944 Paris is liberated from German occupation

Roy Lichtenstein 1923-1997

1946-54 First Indochina War

1910   1915   1920   1925   1930   1935   1940   1945   1950   1952   1954   195

Re 16, Do-Do-Do, Blue, 1960
Private Collection

Yves Klein often painted with sponges instead of paint brushes. Klein liked the sponges so much, he sometimes made them a part of his art. In this work, he attached sponges and pebbles to a flat surface and painted everything in his famous deep blue. What do you think Klein's picture looks like? Could it be the bottom of the sea … or even the surface of the moon?

Good to know:
Like many modern artists, Yves Klein was interested in how people from different parts of the world lived. Klein studied the Japanese sport of judo, which looks like wrestling. He became a master, or expert, at judo.

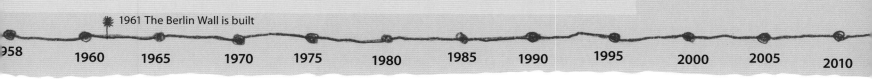
Yves Klein—Blue Sensation

He did something few artists ever do—he created his own color! Klein helped develop a special shade of blue that he used in hundreds of paintings and sculptures.

Sometimes, when you stand in an empty room, you can imagine the things that might be in that room. You can see chairs surrounding a table, green plants by the window, and a cat running across the rug. Yves Klein's art is often like that empty room. It makes you think of things that Klein doesn't actually show you.

Klein made his first important artworks by painting entire canvases in a single color. Each of these paintings, called "monochromes," looked like one big colored rectangle. Klein wanted the people who saw his monochromes to think of people and things that could be in the painting, but weren't.

Klein was also interested in color. For some of his first monochromes, he tried many different colors. But he soon helped develop a deep shade of blue that he liked best. Yves began using this blue in other kinds of art. He made "sculptures" out of blue sponges, blue globes, and even tubs of blue paint. He once had human models make blue creations for him. He covered the models' bodies in blue paint and then had them lie down on blank canvases, where they made big blue "body prints." Klein's color, which he called International Yves Klein Blue, became one of the most famous in modern art!

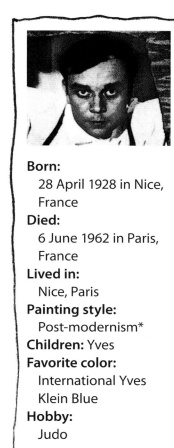

Born:
   28 April 1928 in Nice, France
Died:
   6 June 1962 in Paris, France
Lived in:
   Nice, Paris
Painting style:
   Post-modernism*
Children: Yves
Favorite color:
   International Yves Klein Blue
Hobby:
   Judo

Tip:
You can see many other paintings and sculptures by Yves Klein at the website www.yveskleinarchives.org.

1940 Great Britain defeats Germany in the Battle of Britain

1953 Elizabeth II is crowned queen of the United Kingd

Bridget Riley is born 1931

Dan Flavin 1933-1996

Roy Lichtenstein 1923-1997

1939-45 Second World War

1915 1920 1925 1930 1935 1940 1945 1950 1955 1960 1965 197

Born:
24 April 1931 in London, UK
Lives in:
London, Cornwall, Vaucluse (southern France)
Painting style:
Op Art*

Bridget Riley— What You See Is What You Get

Riley's paintings play tricks on you. In some of them, the lines and shapes seem to be vibrating. In others, it looks as though you could put your hand right into the picture! But these appearances are merely illusions meant to fool your eyes. They are optical illusions*.

Illusions have been around for a long time in art. Look at the old paintings in a museum. They show fruit that looks good enough to eat, clothing that looks soft enough to touch, and horses that seem to be running into the distance. Yet none of these images are real. The artists who painted them used special tricks to make them look real.

Bridget Riley created a special kind of illusion; one that made you think you saw something that couldn't exist in real life. Riley created her optical illusions with simple lines and shapes. She carefully made certain shapes thicker and others thinner, and she made lines that were curved in just the right way. Because she painted so precisely, her pictures often seem to move and vibrate right in front of you! People came to call the art of Bridget Riley and other painters Op Art*. "Op" stands for optical.

Riley's first Op Art pictures were black and white. But later in her career, she painted lines and shapes of many different colors and placed them close together. These colorful paintings seem to shine and flicker on the canvas.

Cataract 3, 1967
British Council Collection

Do you feel uneasy—maybe even seasick—when you look at this picture? Bridget Riley's *Cataract 3* makes its colorful, curving lines look almost like waves on the ocean. Yet, in reality, the painting is perfectly flat and perfectly still!

Tip:
If you like Bridget Riley's paintings, you can visit the website http://kids.niehs.nih.gov/illusion/illusions.htm to see more cool optical illusions.

1939 Early fluorescent lights are used at the New York World's Fair

Dan Flavin 1933-1996

Roy Lichtenstein 1923-1997

Eva Hesse 1936-1970

1939-45 Second World War   1964-75 USA is involved in the Vietnam War

1915   1920   1925   1930   1935   1940   1945   1950   1955   1960   1965   197

Untitled (To Virginia Dwan) I, 1971
Städtische Galerie im Lenbachhaus, Munich

Dan Flavin's art could make beautiful shapes. Do you see the diamond of light behind the fluorescent tube? Look at how the colors in the shape gradually change.

Tip:
The Dan Flavin Art Institute in Bridgehampton, New York, has beautiful examples of the artist's work. Flavin spent many years living in this part of New York.

34

Dan Flavin—Light and Mystery

He was an artist who could paint with light. Flavin's colorful light bulbs could shine on walls, benches, and people, changing the way a room looked and felt.

Born:
  1 April 1933 in
  New York City, USA
Died:
  29 November 1996
  in Riverhead,
  New York, USA
Lived in:
  New York City,
  Garrison-on-Hudson
  (NY), Bridgehampton
  (NY)
Art style:
  Post-modernism*
Children:
  Stephen

Have you been in a room where you can make the lights become gradually brighter or dimmer? Rooms feel different when the light changes. Brightly lit rooms can feel cheerful, while dimly lit rooms can feel mysterious and sometimes scary.

Dan Flavin loved to play with light. He especially liked fluorescent lights— long, thin bulbs that can create many different colors. Dan used these lights in the same way that painters use colored paints.

Flavin carefully placed his fluorescent lights on the walls of museum rooms and other buildings. When the lights were turned on, they lit up the whole room in mysterious ways. If the lights were blue, the room could remind people of a cold evening in a wintry place. If they were green, the room might feel like a warm tropical rain forest. Sometimes Flavin made the light bulbs themselves the most important part of the room, arranging them in beautiful geometric shapes.

You can create your own light art in your bedroom. Take three flashlights and cover their ends with different colored tracing paper. At nighttime, turn off all of the lights in your bedroom. Then shine the covered flashlights on different parts of the ceiling. See what colors and shapes you can make!

An artificial barrier of blue, red and blue fluorescent light (to Flavin Starbuck Judd), 1968

Flavin could make big sculptures by putting his lights together in particular ways. This artwork looks like a red, white, and blue fence; keeping the people on one side of the room from moving to the other side!

1949 West Germany is founded   1961 The Berlin Wall is built

Eva Hesse 1936-1970

Dan Flavin 1933-1996

Joseph Beuys 1921-1986

1939-45 Second World War   1942-45 Millions of Jews killed at the end of the Holocaust

1920   1925   1930   1935   1940   1945   1950   1955   1960   1961   1962   19

Born:
11 January 1936 in Hamburg, Germany

Died:
29 May 1970 in New York City, USA

Lived in:
Hamburg,
New York City

Art style:
Post-minimalism*

Tip:
The website www.evahesse.com has many pictures of Hesse's sculptures and paintings. Take a look!

Eva Hesse—A delicate Artist

She was a sculptor who didn't make art out of marble or bronze. Hesse's creations often look like they could twist and blow away in the wind.

Eva Hesse knew things didn't last forever. She was born in Hamburg, Germany in 1936. But her German childhood didn't last long. She and her Jewish family had to flee their home to escape the German National Socialist government (the Nazis). The Nazis would kill many innocent Jewish families before they were defeated in World War II in 1945.

Hesse's family settled in New York, and Eva studied to become a sculptor. In the 1960s, she returned to Germany with her husband, the sculptor Tom Doyle. They lived for a couple of years in an old factory that had once made textiles for clothes. But this business had not lasted forever. The factory now sat abandoned, except for Eva and Tom. Eva found many interesting things lying around in the factory, including pieces of fabric, rope, and crinkly bits of plastic. She decided to make sculptures out of these thrown-away materials. Soon, she developed a style all her own.

Eva's sculptures are often stringy and soft—like things that won't last forever. Some look like paper-thin clothing that's hanging out to dry in the wind. Others resemble tangled spider's webs or bits of human hair. People admired Eva's work, especially the way she was able to use simple materials to make beautiful and thoughtful art.

Eva soon became famous. But even this success didn't last forever. She died of brain cancer in 1970, at the young age of 34.

No title, 1970
Whitney Museum of American Art, New York

Eva Hesse loved creating art out of ordinary materials. This tangled sculpture is made of rope. What do you think it looks like?

Try to make your own works of art using strings, rope, and old rags. You'll need to use your imagination!

Nichols Canyon, 1980
Private Collection

David Hockney made California his second home. This picture shows a valley in the countryside near Los Angeles. Hockney doesn't paint it exactly as it looked in real life, but he does show us how happy the valley made him feel.

Quiz:
The name of this painting is also the name of the valley it depicts. Can you find this name somewhere in the painting?
(Answer on p. 46)

1984 Los Angeles hosts the Olympic Games   2001 The United States is attacked on 11 September

1987 Andy Warhol, the famous Pop artist, dies   2008 Barack Obama becomes the first African-American to be elected US president

1980   1985   1990   1995   2000   2005   2010   2015   2020   2025   2030   2035

David Hockney—Sun Painting

Hockney loves sunny places, and his paintings often show the bright swimming pools and the wealthy people who live in the sun.

Born:
  9 July 1937 in
  Bradford, England
Lives in:
  London, Los Angeles,
  Bridlington (England)
Painting style:
  Pop Art*
Interest:
  Art history

David Hockney has always been a traveler. He was born in cool, rainy England; but he has lived much of his life in sunny California.

Some of Hockney's best known paintings were made in the 1960s, when he first became an important artist. These pictures show vast California swimming pools alongside houses with huge windows. Hockney used new acrylic paints* to create the bright colors that he saw on a sunny California day. Sometimes his paintings show funny things, like a mysterious splash in a pool. Other Hockney paintings show wealthy people, many of whom have lived in the kinds of California homes that David made famous.

Hockney also loves photography, and he has become well known for his photocollages*. He creates them by taking many different photographs of a place or object, and then putting the photos together in a way that makes the original place or object look unusual. In one of Hockney's photocollages, a city street looks like it has been hit by an earthquake. All the buildings and cars seem to be cracked up!

Try making your own photocollage. Take photographs of different parts of your house, and then paste the pictures together on a big piece of paper. See what kind of picture you can create!

Tip:
Look for more David Hockney paintings and photographs at the website www.hockneypictures.com.

A Bigger Splash, 1967
Tate Britain, London

Someone has just jumped into a
quiet swimming pool, and the
splash looks like a big explosion!
But Hockney doesn't show us
the person who made the splash.
That person is now under the water.

Glossary

ABSTRACT EXPRESSIONISM is a style of painting that uses shapes, lines, and other "abstract" forms that do not represent real things. Abstract Expressionists make art that "expresses," or shows, their thoughts and feelings.

ACRYLIC PAINT is a kind of paint that artists began using in the 1950s. It dries quickly and can make unusually bright colors. Many Pop Artists*, including David Hockney, have painted with acrylic paints.

CANVAS is a strong type of fabric on which artists make paintings. Canvases often come stretched out on a wooden frame.

COLLAGE is a type of art in which different objects are placed together in a particular way to make a single image. Many collages combine things that don't normally belong together.

CUBISM is a style of painting that shows people and objects "broken up" into geometric shapes. Sometimes, Cubists portray an object from several different angles at the same time.

DADAISM is a style of art that rejects things that other people find normal. Dadaists often create art that makes fun of normal life. Like Surrealism*, Dadaism may take ordinary objects and make them look unusual or funny. The first Dadaists chose the silly word "Dada" on purpose to describe their art.

EXPRESSIONISM is an art style that began during the early 1900s. Artists that work in this style use their art to "express," or show, their feelings and ideas. Expressionists do not portray things exactly as they appear in real life. Instead, they change the shapes of these things, and they often use bold, unrealistic colors.

IMMIGRANT is a person who moves from one country in order to make a new home in another country. During the late 1800s and early 1900s, thousands of people from Europe immigrated to the United States. Many moved to America to find work, while others fled their countries to escape governments that were taking away their freedom.

MOSAIC is a picture made up of tiny pieces of colored stone, glass, or other material. Mosaic artists carefully arrange the little pieces together and attach them to a hard surface. From a distance, some mosaics look just like paintings!

OP ART is a style of art that uses optical illusion*.

OPTICAL ILLUSION is a picture made to fool your eyes. In some paintings that use optical illusion, the lines are painted in a way that makes them seem to be quivering. Yet, in reality, they are perfectly still.

PERFORMANCE ART is a kind of art that is "performed," or acted out, by people.

Beginning in the 1960s, Joseph Beuys and others helped make performance art popular.

PHOTOCOLLAGE is a type of collage* in which several photographs are placed together to make one large picture. Photocollages often use many different photos of a single object, person, or place.

POP ART "Pop" stands for "popular," and Pop Artists typically show people and things that are well-loved and easily understood. For example, they may portray comic book scenes, movie stars, or even soup cans!

POST-MINIMALISM is an art style that is part of a larger art movement called Post-modernism*. Many Post-minimalists are sculptors who use ordinary materials to create complex shapes.

POST-MODERNISM means "after Modernism." From the 1920s through the 1950s, Modernism was the most important style of art. Modernists often created artworks that were not meant to represent real people or things. Some of the best known Modernists were the Abstract Expressionists*. During the 1950s, young artists began making new works that looked different from Modernist art. Many of these "Post-modernists" decided to paint real people and objects again. Pop Art* is a type of Post-modernism.

REALISM is a style of art that tries to portray people and things as they appear in real life. Realist painters, like Edward Hopper, use colors to show how sunlight makes shadows and beautiful colors. These artists also create realistic looking spaces.

SURREALISM is an art style that takes familiar objects and presents them in an unfamiliar way. Some Surrealists combine things that don't normally go together. Others try to make ordinary objects look like something they're not. Surrealist artworks often seem mysterious, dreamlike, or even funny.

Answers to the quiz questions

Page 10: Marc Chagall's father worked as a fish seller, so Chagall often put fish in his paintings.

Page 24: Joseph Beuys and his helpers took about five years to plant the 7,000 trees in Kassel.

Page 40: Nichols Canyon. In the middle of the painting, Hockney labels the black street "Nichols Cyn Rd," which is short for "Nichols Canyon Road.

Library of Congress Control Number: 2009942267; British Library Cataloguing-in-Publication Data: a catalogue record for this book is available from the British Library; Deutsche Nationalbibliothek holds a record of this publication in the Deutsche Nationalbibliografie; detailed bibliographical data can be found under: http://dnb.d-nb.de

Portraits:
Pablo Picasso with his Dalmatian, photograph by Edward Quinn; Marcel Duchamp, 1965, photograph by Ugo Mulas; Marc Chagall, photograph by Franz Hubmann; Edward Hopper in Cape Elizabeth, Maine, 1927, photograph; Alexander Calder with his circus, 1929, photograph by André Kertész; Mark Rothko in front of No. 7, 1961, photograph; Joseph Beuys, photograph; Roy Lichtenstein, photograph by Laurie Lamprecht; Yves Klein, photograph by Harry Shunk; Bridget Riley, 1971, photograph by Angelika Platen; Dan Flavin, photograph; Eva Hesse with An Ear in a Pond, photograph by Manfred Tischer; David Hockney, photograph, Camera Press / Interfoto.

Picture credits:
Akg: p. 7; bpk: p. 23; laif: p. 25; Tate Images: pp. 42-3; ullstein bild: pp. 24, 36-7; Whitney Museum of American Art: pp. 18-9, 39.

Front cover: Details taken from works by Lichtenstein (p. 26), Riley (p. 33), Hopper (p. 13).
Frontispiece: Detail taken from a work by Hopper (pp. 14-5).

Prestel books are available worldwide. Please contact your nearest bookseller or one of the following addresses for information concerning your local distributor.

Prestel Verlag, Munich
a member of Verlagsgruppe Random House GmbH
www.prestel.de

Prestel Publishing Ltd.
14-17 Wells Street
London W1T 3PD

Prestel Publishing
900 Broadway, Suite 603
New York, NY 10003
www.prestel.com

Project Management: Doris Kutschbach, Larissa Spicker
Picture Editor: Larissa Spicker
Copyediting: Cynthia Hall
Design: Michael Schmölzl, agenten.und.freunde, Munich
Art Direction: Cilly Klotz
Production: Astrid Wedemeyer
Origination: ReproLine mediateam, Munich
Printing and Binding: Printer Trento, Trento

Verlagsgruppe Random House FSC® N001967
The FSC®-certified paper Profibulk has been supplied by Igepa.

ISBN 978-3-7913-7015-6